AF176098

Daniel McCosh

Da Capo

Bibliografische Information der Deutschen Nationalbibliothek:
Die Deutsche Nationalbibliothek verzeichnet diese Publikation in der
Deutschen Nationalbibliografie; detaillierte bibliografische Daten sind im
Internet über http://dnb.dnb.de abrufbar.

Cover and Design: Claudia Habermann & Daniel McCosh

Herstellung und Verlag: BoD – Books on Demand, Norderstedt

ISBN: 978-3-7519-3004-8

Public Service Announcement

As the radio crackled into life
(It had been sadly forgotten in the corner
After the war, tubes and valves
And lessons learned sadly neglected)
Voices from the past whispered from its dusty circuits

The people are called upon
To show their strength, their resilience
And embrace the nature within
The true DNA that builds families
And homes; that connects us all

This voice is mine now and it
Pleads for calm and reason as we prepare to hibernate
Remember now the pleasure of a bed sheet
And two rickety chairs
How we could turn it into a castle with a snap
And build our own kingdom

As we pile the cushions high now
We can return to our children's dreams
Remember all that we have forgotten
So that when the time comes to rebuild and mend
We have the power to make it better

The voice on the radio drones on, it belongs to another
I've no time for the old rulers
Just a sharpener and pencil in my hand
And a single sheet to set out
A new plan to how we can live and love now

No time to pad my nest with toilet paper
And fill my cupboards while others go hungry
No time to keep up with an endless news cycle
Distracting us from what we can do now
In our homes
To fix and grow
Sunflower seeds

Sunflowers on my Telefunken

Sunflowers on my Telefunken
Wearing my pink shades
The ones with the thick rims
Disco leopard with the sequin ears
And a box of tissues for hard times

Not worried about the glitch
In the picture
It's probably the chlorophyll again
Getting in the circuits and cathode ray tubes
Or the lichen that sprouted suddenly on Tuesday
Through the cracks in the glass

I found it in a skip, brought it home and tended to it
The picture grew stronger day after day
I couldn't have found a better flower pot
Now I have sunflowers on my Telefunken
Stuck on Channel 8, just after the white noise

If You're Human You Should Know It

If you're human you should know it
Wash your hands
If you're human you should know it
Wash your hands
If you care and you know it
And you really want to show it
If you're human and you know it
Wash your hands

(If you're German and you know it
And you really want to show it
Wash your Hans)

Civilisation

When it comes to the crunch
We are an amusing species
Rather than sully our hands
With a mess of our own making

We lament the scarcity
Of a bizarre commodity
It's become a bizarre comedy
Of a civilisation caught short

I raise my hand and salute you
With a clean but angry finger
Should you find yourself in a delicate circumstance
You may use this page

Doctor Doctor

I feel funny
Call the doctor
Who do doctors call?
Do they call funny men?
Eat an apple
And stay all day in bed?

Doctor doctor
If my nose runs
And my feet smell
Has the world
Turned upside down?

Doctor doctor
Are you feeling OK?
We are all so grateful
That you are there
Every day

Lifeline

Hissing
Silence
Steady
Breath
4000
Times
In
An
Eerie
Night
-ingale
Wing
Day
After
Day
They
Rest
I
Hope
They
Live

Purse Strings

Clap
Clap

No more
Of your
Clap
Trap

The people
Have had enough
Of your...

Let the people
Clap you out

And leave the WHO,
And the what and the when
To the people
Who know HOW

Protecting Our Own

Read leaders the riot act
Scorn their blood money
My etched face is bleeding
They waited for too long
There are parasitic adversaries
Worse than a virus
And broken systems
Give me protein and a Glockenspiel
I am sick
But I will save them first
And play myself out

Carrying on for Nigel

When we're out of fresh produce
We'll need fresh ideas
When our hair grows too long
We'll need to get a buzz
From our own cuts and styles
Soon we'll need a lot of things
We had but took for granted
But we will find new ways
To carry on as stalwart primates
With tea and chimpathy

Stunned

I couldn't remember the word when I felt it
Sliding back into my tortoise-shell rollneck
As I rubbernecked helplessly
Wishing the news would unfold like a newspaper
Slowly and comfortably over breakfast

Headline-stunned, funny that, fraidy cat
Too frit to scat when bright lights come :-
Colour and the feeling passes - poised -
Ready for the next move
It came back to me (shell-shocked)
But that was another war
Now the news is our enemy
And we can move faster than we think
When it counts, the time to act is now

This was a home-made hand grenade
We'll remember one day
There's more than one way to make lemonade
And it's worth being afraid of yellow

Plans on Ice

In a place where we met in happier times
Now the fear of a make-shift morgue
Cooling our bodies
Let's hope they won't reclaim the stadiums
Not for sport's sake
But for a love of one another

The rink is closed now
Steel blue flashes from a figure skater's blades
Sparks carving memories in the darkness
This graceful und unseemly smith
Pirouettes into a colourful finale

Divas and Legends

She's on the
Golden spotlight staircase
Pretty's on the showgirl drums
Thrashing her in. The Diva
Throws back her wild mane
Mouth gaping, the sound escaping
So tidal glowing almost bridal
Underneath the starlight stutter
The Diva is a moaner and a screecher
A sonic mona lisa
Her lashes glitter

Side stage, he enters with a
Saw tooth and a throaty roar
Head buzzing ready to rock
The legend is a cowboy
Laying his hat down in the ring
In a duet of two powerful voices
The Diva and the Legend
A match made in heaven

Little Tinkers

Close the windows
Toss out the bad apple
Drop the tabs
Run to the trail
Leave it all behind

Big thinkers
Little thinkers
Round thinkers
Square thinkers
Oh you, little tinkers
With no blinkers
Staring life in the mouth

Itchy Sketches

In the 1980s
I drew bright red pictures
With mosquito legs
I called them
Itchy sketches
I was a horrid child

Invisible Tramlines

Moss spurned forth from tenement ashes
Spores in the lungs of graffiti shadowed youth
Echo thundering of a passing train
Resonance of an urban sprawl
A breathless choked ecosystem
Spray-painted souls stifled by the fumes
Chemical cities masked by disinfectant
Simple words please simple minds the party Politik
But the communities will rise from
The acid terraces and dilute the concrete
With seeds of compassion
Vests stained with the stench of honest work and stewed
tea
The weak building bridges on the backs of the strong
Same as it ever was
The people held together by voltage and tramlines
In the darkest times, stars will line the sky.

Lightning Conductor

A ticket to ride, the devil's streetcar
The lightning conductor with the golden crowns
Never sure whether to be
Fearful of his Dremel gaze
Driving through the ratchets and rivets
Of the very skeleton

Oh he turns the dead man's switch
Cackles spit flecking steel
Sparks of a working man's city
Landing on dogged lapels

He is struck
Lightning shreds the sprockets
The steel screeches
We slide into darkness

Telegraph

Buzzing through the telegraph wires
Gyrating molar patterns
Disrupting cavities and
So many chattering teeth
Sending messages, sending
Telegrams for lifeforms

Charring the crow's feathers
Perching precariously, the precarious
Purchasing and soul sales at 100 percent
Humanity glowing white hot in the angry wires
Bring back the lovers
Let them kiss and play
We are all birds of a feather

These Four Walls

Face-to-face is yesterday's game
And online presence is the new test screen
Staying inside is testing our nature, while nature thrives
From social dancing to social distancing
'Is' a difference of two letters plus the 't'
We can no longer share with a friend
Calm observations, not complaints
These four walls protect and inspire
Where others see constraints

On the balance of things
Hanging in the balance
Like an online checking account
Poetry may seem to have little value
But there are enough notebooks to feed
Everyone
And learning to think again
Is our new currency anyway
Let's invest in our futures
Safe and sound in these four walls

Barbie's House

Pastel colours are easier on the eye
And there is room for happy families
The dolls lie blissfully lifeless
In their plastic cribs with pretty painted on faces
Wash my hair in the sink
And set me down in my best dress
There is a pleasant breeze
And we can change the furniture every day
If we get bored of the same
Picture on the television
Contained and blissful
With every accessory we need
But our friends and
Our lives outside the box

Contessa

Click clack
I am Hercules,
The traveller
Of Olympia
A German
Contessa
With
An eagle
At my shoulder
Click
Clack
Ping
I write
As the candle
Wax drips
On
The Contessa's
Orange
Lips
A
Carbon
Copy
Click
Clack
Click

Born to Bongo

Bingo!
I'll bang bongos
Not Ringo's bongos
Or dingo bongos
Or flamingo bongo
Or bunga bunga bongos
Just my bongos
Under the palms

Bingo!
Bongo jingles!
Little one, big one
Back and forth
Bum bum bum
Tum tum tum

Needlework

A stitch in time would have
Saved nine, but the people
Will make do and mend
Patiently sewing another patch
From the rocker
Such fine needlework that can
Hold our families together now

Thread a needle
And strike it deep into the system
A thread to strengthen
The seat of their pants
In danger of ripping at the seams
Embarrassing our leaders

Madeleine

Madeleine
Make the tea
Teach them songs
About you and me

Songs about
Right and wrong
Making do and
Making them believe

Clap your hands
Madeleine

Now you know what you know
You can come home

I've seen our future
And I'm frozen
To the bone

Now you know what you know
You can come home

When I read that book
Make up for lost time
That's when I'll know you
Madeleine

We'll make your cake
When the air is clean
We'll sing your rainbow
When you can tell
Grey from green

When I read that book
Make up for lost time
That's when I'll know you
My Madeleine

Sandstorm

And they rise
Sand castles
In the desert
Air locked inside
As they rise
In the sandstorm
Only dust
And barely light
Inside
Sand blasting
Outside and still
Their lungs rise
A new desire
Keeps them alive
One day
The sand masses
Will taste sweet
Again

Around the House in Eighty Ways

0	20
A skater	A Monday
A dancer	A Tuesday
A mover	A Wednesday
A shaker	A Thursday
A pilot	A Friday
A jet-skier	A Saturday
A Kabarettist	A Sunday
A Carabinieri	A goldfish
A coachman	A starfish
A gaslighter	A shellfish
10	30
A footman	A crab
A fighter	A wizard
A rower	A witch
A runner	A monster
A jogger	A raincloud
A walker	A king
A clown	A queen
A talker	A princess
A sunray	A prince
A sailor	A season

40
A dream
A nightmare
A molecule
A particle
A cuticle
A marionette
A majorette
A tiger
A dunebug
A ladybird
50
A ventricle
A spider
A fly
A mosquito
A beetle
A lizard
A chameleon
A crocodile
A spell
A curse

60
A wonder
A miracle
A ruler
A saviour
A flowerpot
A nightingale
A hummingbird
A honeypot
A teapot
A florist
70
A butcher
A baker
A candle-stick maker
A bell
A needle
A thread
A killjoy
A makejoy
A saint
A believer of
ANYTHING

Bittersweet

Bittersweet
Chocolate treat
So fine to eat
The finest gentleman
Melting on the tongue

Blue Print

When schematics get
erratic
And heretics dramatic

Smear it blue
Right it new, alight and
skew
Attenuate and slew

A fourth dimension

It's printed in blue
No more black and white
For you
No more black and blue

For you
It's printed in blue
For you

To follow these footsteps

It's time to lead now
Pull out the wires
And break the circuits

Blow a fuse
No more black and blue
For you
So forget the news
Do what you got to do

Faulty Circuits

With all the diagnostics available to modern science
The whitecoats try mesmerism, magnetism, scintillation
and finally:
Gas chromatography
To separate the emotions
And spectrographic colonoscopies
A purge the likes of which man has never seen

Tweaking and adjusting mathematical models
Unable to fathom quantum potentials
In faulty organic circuits.
The spontaneous eruptions of living matter
Insoluble to chemical attempts to saturate
Beautiful hopes and dreams:
Art transpiring through faulty circuits

Schu-bert, yeah!

Impervious to the wall of sound resonating
In exuberance from Schubert's finesse
The needle scratches deep into the grooves
Seeking purchase until the surface cracks
Shellac is a beautiful word
If you only could hear it
But Monday came and the same broken record
Shellac, shellac, shellac
What a dreadfully morose chap!
If you'd dust between the sleeves of the long plays
The petunias would thank you with a fog horn of colour
No but, Schu-bert, yeah

Franz in the Irrgarten

From the study window the harpsichord drones, ave
Maria
There are no aeroplanes overhead
Perched on wrought iron doilies
We take our tea and breathe the country air

'I do wonder what Franz would have thought about hip-
hop,'
He murmured through yellowing teeth
To no one in particular
And lapsed back into a dream of labyrinths
With amazing grace

Mind Music

What a mother load
32 precisely
And a Korg with it's creamy monologues
So many musical stories to tell
My friend Roland
And make him Yamaha-ha
I'll make mind music with the latest
Cerebral modules
From grey matter
Hey Mr Pitch Shifter
Be careful with that PIANO
It's patched to a classical universe
(Controlled by a PIANIST)

Death of a Casio in D Flat

Da da d_
A melody cursed
More frightening
Than a toothless grandmother
Percussive flatulence
In a plastic can
But da, da, da
Got them rocking
Natty, nasty
Demo song
Da, da, whoa
Battery low
Calculator in crisis
Going slow
Its
temperamental
tempo
Lost
In
A
Heartbeat and a
FLICKER
From its LCD soul

You'll never play alone, dear VL-tone
We'll jam together in Silicon Hell

Histrionic Harmonics

Histrionic harmonics
The enigmatic mathematical mayhem
Of signals processed in space
Scatter patterns and spectrographs
Black holes spin white noise
White dwarfs, blue dwarfs, red dwarfs
A bigger bang

Welcome to the universe
Space is spectral
Space is phenomenon
Space is radiant
Space is ambient
Space is quantum
Space is noise

We are in orbit now
We are in the stars
We are in orbit now
We are in the stars

Satellite solar flare
Scatter your matter
Through space rhythm
Dots on my oscilloscope
Telescope

We are in orbit now
Getting spaced
Finding our space
There is space
For everyone

Librarians

Dangerous talk of
Lustful flowers
And whiling away
The gentle hours
With sweet plums
And fingered flutes
Excuse me young man
Those books are not
For children
The librarian
Touched herself
Between the stacks
As he leaves
Red cheeks glowering
Defiantly
Never trust a librarian

Palm Trees

A storm ripped through the complex
We weren't surprised, the rock star palms
Made heavenly headbangers as we watched
Safe on the inside

They said it was an unconventional choice
To wear palm trees but
Now you hold them close to your heart
You always picked flowers over mosquitos
And ate raspberries with your popcorn

I am Spartacus

I am Spartacus
The sunshine child
No, I am Spartacus
The mad, the wild
We are Spartacus
The free, the strong
They are Spartacus
The mighty, the loyal
She is Spartacus
The leader the one
He is Spartacus
The light, the sun
Crucify them all
To pacify the few

Reclaimed

Lichen etched into the stone
Tears; linear expressions of hope and sadness
Entrenched in faces waiting in stony silence
When humanity crumbles, nature reclaims

Sculpted and raised by masterful hands
An artful existence upon a marble arch
Ivory smiles and broken wings
The years may be unkind for mortals
But angels will carry them home

forskellige ting

You take what a man writes
Forsake that young man a life
No final interpretation is ever right
It's really about many things

Love
Humour
Human
Honesty
Anger

But if it fits your agenda
Make it about religion, politics
And destroy a human

Do we choose to be poets?
Yes, I read books
So do other people
Stealing that moped
Was a happy accident

Love
Humour
Human
Honesty
Anger

Found me grounded
Now I rest my soul
I have taught you
forskellige ting